FAMOUS MOVIE MONSTERS ™

INTRODUCING
THE DEADLY MANTIS

The Rosen Publishing Group, Inc.,
New York

GENEVIEVE RAJEWSKI

For my parents, who always let me watch the Creature Double Feature*, and Nathan, my movie date*

Published in 2007 by The Rosen Publishing Group, Inc.
29 East 21st Street, New York, NY 10010

First Edition

Library of Congress Cataloging-in-Publication Data

Rajewski, Genevieve.
Introducing the deadly mantis/Genevieve Rajewski.—1st ed.
    p. cm.—(Famous movie monsters)
Includes bibliographical references and index.
ISBN 1-4042-0848-8 (library binding)
1. Deadly mantis (Motion picture: 1957) I. Title. II. Series.
PN1997.D377R35 2007
791.43—dc22
                                                              2006000046

Manufactured in Malaysia

On the Cover: This image of the giant mantis is from a 1957 advertisement for the film.

CONTENTS

CHAPTER 1

THE DEADLY MANTIS

An erupting volcano causes glaciers to thaw, and huge expanses of ice crash into the freezing waters near the North Pole. From deep within the melting ice, a prehistoric creature begins to stir.

South of the North Pole is Red Eagle One, a military base and control center for the Distant Early Warning (DEW) line. The DEW line is a radar system that protects America against sneak attacks. Weather Four is the name of a small outpost of the DEW line. The two men working there are going about their normal routine when they see a blip on their radar screen. As they try to figure out what the blip might indicate, they hear a loud buzzing noise outside. Suddenly, the windows of the building blow out and the ceiling caves in.

Soon afterward, a pilot spots the damaged weather shack from the air. He radios Red Eagle One to say that he is worried that the shack's inhabitants might be hurt. Colonel Joe Parkman, the officer in charge of Red Eagle One, sets off by plane to investigate.

When Colonel Parkman arrives at Weather Four, the shack is eerily quiet and badly damaged. Both of the men who were working there have vanished. Colonel Parkman doesn't understand what happened. Everything was normal when the missing men last checked in with Red Eagle One. There has been no storm that could have damaged the shack. Although the sides of the building are caved out as though something crashed into the roof, there is no sign of a plane crash, and there are no bodies.

Hoping that the men may have set off on foot for Red Eagle One, Colonel Parkman looks for footprints in the snow. Instead, he finds a deep track, as if something had come in for a landing. However, the track is too short for an airplane landing and too deep to have been caused by a helicopter.

Hours later, back at Red Eagle One, a strange blip appears on the radar screen. Colonel Parkman sends several jets to look for anything unusual. Soon, the blip disappears, and the jets are called back. However, one C-47 cargo plane will never have the chance to return. Its pilots hear a loud buzzing sound just seconds before something crashes into the plane, sending it plummeting to the frozen earth below.

A jet pilot returning to Red Eagle One spots the wreckage of the C-47. Once again, Colonel Parkman investigates. At the crash site, he finds a track in the snow identical to the one seen at the destroyed weather shack. Again, there are no bodies.

Suddenly, a large object crashes through the plane's ceiling, narrowly missing the colonel. The strange object is sharp, and it appears to be a fragment of something far larger. Colonel Parkman brings it back to the base and calls the Pentagon.

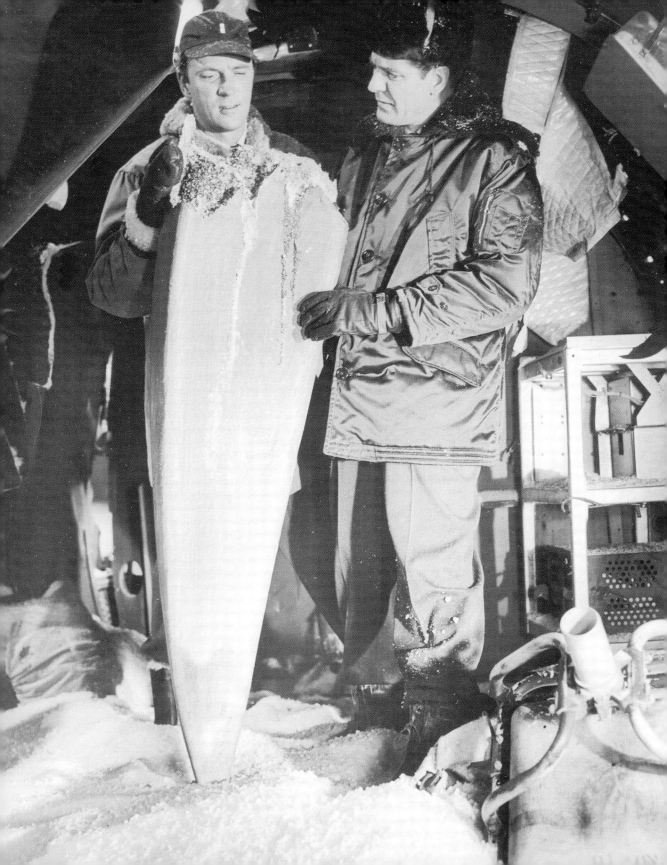

In Washington, D.C., General Mark Ford calls a meeting of scientific experts to discuss the mysterious object. After two days of study, the experts agree that it is an appendage of a living creature. However, they cannot figure out what kind of living creature the appendage might have been a part of, as it is not from any known Arctic animal. Running out of options, they decide to ask Dr. Ned Jackson, a paleontologist at Washington's Museum of Natural History, for help.

Ned is meeting with Marge Blaine, the editor of the museum magazine, when he gets the Pentagon's call. A former news reporter, Marge presses Ned about why the Pentagon is calling. Ned tells her the government wants to know more about an old bone found up at the North Pole.

At the Pentagon, Ned examines the object and determines that it is not a bone. He suspects that the object is part of an insect and orders a laboratory test to confirm this.

Back at the museum, Marge tells Ned that she has figured out that the "bone" he is researching has something to do with the recent disappearances in the Arctic. Ned confides that this is true and sketches a picture of the green, five-foot-long body part. Marge remarks that it looks like the spur on a grasshopper or a cricket. Ned agrees, but notes that grasshoppers are not meat eaters and that at least five men have disappeared.

Colonel Parkman (Craig Stevens) *(right)* and another officer are astonished by the size of the mysterious object, which resembles a fang or a claw. Scenes like these were common in monster movies. They were a way of building suspense by getting the audience to imagine what kind of creature such an appendage might belong to.

This conversation leads Ned to a seemingly impossible conclusion, which he soon shares with General Ford. Ned believes that the object is the spur from the foreleg of a gigantic prehistoric praying mantis. "As large as the creature is we're looking for, I doubt anything could be as deadly," Ned warns. "It's strong. It walks, leaps, and flies. Its appetite is insatiable. In all the kingdom of the living, there is no more deadly or voracious creature than the praying mantis."

The American military is skeptical about the existence of a monster praying mantis, but Eskimos in Greenland are about to discover it is real. An Eskimoan village is overcome by a loud buzzing sound. Suddenly, a gigantic mantis appears on the horizon. The creature roars and rears above two doomed villagers. Its enormous spurred forelegs block out the sun.

After word of the attack reaches the Pentagon, Ned departs for Red Eagle One. Marge invites herself along as his photographer. At the base, they meet Colonel Parkman. The trio spends the day at the scene of the first attack and then returns to the base, where a party is in progress. Unknown to the officers dancing inside, the mantis is creeping up on the base, its eyes glowing in the darkness.

Meanwhile, Ned is trying to figure out how big the mantis is. He concludes that it is from an era when the smallest insects were as big as men. Marge screams as she spies the mantis peering through the window. The mantis responds by piercing the roof with one of its forelegs, and the ceiling begins to cave in! As Colonel Parkman, Marge, and Ned run through the rubble to safety, officers fire at the mantis with flamethrowers and machine guns. The bloodthirsty mantis flies away unharmed.

In this colorized advertisement for *The Deadly Mantis,* Colonel Parkman stands near a picture of an enormous praying mantis. Craig Stevens, the actor who played Colonel Parkman in *The Deadly Mantis,* would go on to have a successful career in television.

Colonel Parkman, Ned, and Marge head back to Washington to warn the nation about the mantis. An unexplained attack on a freight boat leads the team to deduce that the mantis is heading due south at more than 200 miles (320 kilometers) per hour. At that speed, the mantis will soon be over the United States! Colonel Parkman and Ned call upon the Ground Observer Corps volunteers to report any unusual sightings.

A civilian volunteer's tip sends jets off in pursuit of the flying mantis. The mantis is hit with rockets and drops out of sight, but because of heavy fog, the fighter pilots cannot confirm whether or not they killed the monster.

Meanwhile, Marge comes up with the clever idea to track the mantis. She uses news reports to mark recent unusual occurrences on a map of the United States. She keeps at her work until well after midnight, when the colonel insists he give her a ride home. On the car radio, they hear that a train engine and five cars have overturned only a few miles away. They visit the scene of the wreckage, but decide it is just an accident caused by the fog. They do not notice the telltale mantis track in the dirt nearby.

The recent scare inspires Colonel Parkman to kiss Marge in his car. While they are distracted by their feelings for each other, the mantis claims new victims across town. The monster appears out of nowhere to stab a bus with its foreleg and smash it to the ground. Colonel Parkman and Marge hear on the car radio that a bus has just been demolished and there are no bodies. The announcer says the event is the seventh unexplained local accident in just twenty-four hours.

Colonel Parkman and Marge's suspicions are soon confirmed. The mantis has been sighted over Washington! The monster manages to avoid missile fire as it flies over the Capitol. It slowly scales the Washington Monument, roaring at the city before taking to the sky once more.

Jets pursue the mantis as it flies northeast. It drops below the radar network, but one alert woman sights the mantis in New Jersey. Led by Colonel Parkman, fighter jets chase the

As seen in this colorized still from the film, a showdown is set to occur as soldiers prepare to battle the dangerous mantis. As in many movies featuring giant monsters, a large group of people have banded together to try to stop the monster's rampage. They want to prevent the mantis from flooding the city by destroying the tunnel where it is trapped.

mantis, firing continuously. Nothing stops the monster, so Colonel Parkman crashes his jet into it, parachuting out of the cockpit at the last minute. The wounded mantis staggers toward New York City, where it hides itself in a traffic tunnel.

The area around the tunnel is chaotic. Ned says that the mantis will die from the injury caused by the jet crash. However, the dying monster could still break through the tunnel walls and cause a flood. Colonel Parkman decides to lead soldiers into the tunnel, using smoke as a cover. They all wear gas masks to protect themselves from the chemical mines they are carrying, which should kill the mantis if they can just get close enough to use them.

Inside the dark and smoky tunnel, the soldiers' flashlights reveal overturned cars. The men hear a fierce, screamlike roar. Suddenly, the mantis rears above them. The soldiers fire their guns, and the monster hurls several cars at them. Colonel Parkman launches the first of the chemical mines. The gas causes the mantis to waver, but the wheezing monster marches closer. The colonel throws another mine. The wounded mantis screeches in pain and throws another car. Then, gasping, the mantis teeters and slowly crumples to the tunnel's floor.

The battle finally over, Colonel Parkman brings Ned, Marge, and General Ford to the dead mantis. As Marge photographs the scene, the mantis slowly raises a foreleg above her. Colonel Parkman sees what is about to happen and pushes her out of harm's way just in time.

Fortunately, the beast is, indeed, dead. The movement was just a muscle spasm. Colonel Parkman and Marge embrace as the rest of the group laugh in relief.

THE MAKING OF THE DEADLY MANTIS

Originally released in 1957, *The Deadly Mantis* is a typical Hollywood monster movie from that era. Although entertaining, there was nothing groundbreaking about the film. The screenwriter and producer based the story on the plot of another successful monster movie called *Them!* (1954). Existing black-and-white footage provided by the U.S. military was pieced together to create many scenes. While director Nathan Juran had a reputation for working on science fiction films, *The Deadly Mantis* is not one of his more well known efforts.

THEM!

The idea for *The Deadly Mantis* began with the movie *Them!*. Released in 1954, *Them!* thrilled audiences by combining the elements of science fiction with a murder mystery. The story begins with a girl who is found wandering the desert alone. She is the sole survivor of unknown attackers who have killed her family. When asked who committed the crime,

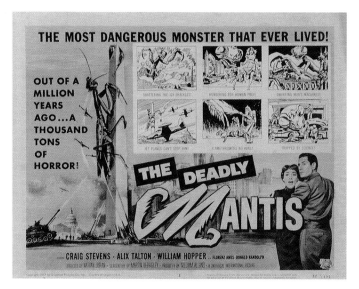

An original poster for the movie uses dramatic illustrations to arouse public interest. If a monster movie was poorly produced or cheaply made, the filmmakers often had to rely on an exciting poster to get people to come see the movie. Many old movie posters are now appreciated for their artistic elements.

all she can utter is, *"Them!"* As the movie unfolds, disappearances in the area increase. Strange tracks are found in the desert sand, and someone or something is ransacking the town for sugar. Two entomologists finally trace the attacks to giant ants mutated by radioactive testing. The outlandish ants of *Them!* terrified audiences, and soon a number of movies were released featuring giant animals or insects as the villains.

Them! was a big moneymaker at the box office. Producer William Alland and screenwriter Martin Berkeley used the plot of *Them!* as a road map for Universal Studio's production of *The Deadly Mantis*. This formula resulted in another mystery with missing bodies, a clever scientist, and a giant insect. The writers decided on their monster after seeing a preserved praying mantis at the Los Angeles Museum of Science and Industry in 1956.

STOCK FOOTAGE

Like many 1950s horror films, *The Deadly Mantis* was produced quickly and inexpensively. This meant that there was

THE REAL-LIFE DEADLY MANTIS

William Alland and Martin Berkeley's decision to cast a praying mantis as a deadly monster was a smart one.

"The mantis looks like a killer, because it is a killer," says May Berenbaum, head of the Entomology Department at the University of Illinois at Urbana-Champaign. "Mantids are very efficient predators that are adept at snagging just about every conceivable type of prey. Most predators leave bees and wasps alone, but mantids have no problem eating them. They also can eat a lot of poisonous species."

In the tropics, large mantises have also been known to eat lizards, hummingbirds, and small frogs. Baby mantises will cannibalize each other if there is no other food source, and female mantises frequently decapitate their male partners during mating.

Two to four inches (5–10 centimeters) long, a mantis assumes its "praying position" while lying in wait for prey. It holds its front legs tight to its body while anchoring itself to a stem or branch with its back and middle legs. The mantis strikes in the blink of an eye, impaling its victims on the spurs of its forelegs.

The mantis' strike is so deadly that a style of kung fu (T'ang L'ang Ch'uan) has been based on it. Legend has it that a Chinese monk saw a praying mantis fight and defeat a cicada. He was so impressed by how the mantis used its forelegs to overcome this much larger opponent that he took notes on how the insect protected itself. The monk then used the foreleg movements to create a new, powerful form of kung fu fighting.

A praying mantis prepares to devour its latest victim.

no time or money to film many scenes on location. As a result, some of *The Deadly Mantis* was put together using what is called stock footage, or film footage shot for another purpose.

For example, scenes of an Eskimo fleeing the mantis are taken from a movie called *S.O.S. Eisberg*. This 1933 German film about a group that goes in search of a missing Arctic explorer was filmed on location in Greenland. Universal owned the rights to *S.O.S. Eisberg*, so it was easy to reuse the Arctic scenes for *The Deadly Mantis*.

The Deadly Mantis also uses a lot of stock footage from the United States military. In the 1950s, the military often let movie studios use such footage because it presented a favorable image of the armed forces to the public. *The Deadly Mantis* has many examples of military stock footage, including shots of the USS *Antietam*, a CV-36 aircraft carrier.

THE DIRECTOR

Nathan Juran, director of *The Deadly Mantis*, earned an Academy Award for his art direction on the film *How Green Was My Valley* (1941). However, he is best known for his work on science fiction films, such as *Attack of the 50 Foot Woman* (1958) and *The Brain from Planet Arous* (1957).

Juran did some fine work with Ray Harryhausen, a famous special-effects artist. Together, they filmed *20 Million Miles to Earth* (1957), about a giant Venusian alien, and *The 7th Voyage of Sinbad* (1958), a fantasy movie that has influenced numerous other movies and television shows.

When working on a badly produced film, Juran would often use the pseudonym Nathan Hertz or Jerry Juran to protect his reputation. In Tom Weaver's book *Attack of the Monster Movie Makers: Interviews with 20 Genre Giants*, producer Jacques Marquette says Juran did this because "he didn't want people to know that he would make that cheap a picture."

CASTING

When *The Deadly Mantis* was announced in 1956, Rex Reason was billed as its star. Reason had just starred in the intergalactic adventure film *This Island Earth* (1955), a science fiction block-buster, and *The Deadly Mantis* script left him unimpressed.

Nathan Juran *(left)* and Boris Karloff *(right)* rehearse the script for *The Black Castle* in 1952. Boris Karloff, famous for his starring role as the monster in *Frankenstein* (1931), starred in many horror films. Juran was an architect before he was a director. His film career began when he made a drawing for a movie studio.

"To me it was very corny," said Reason in Mark A. Vieiria's book *Hollywood Horror: From Gothic to Cosmic*. "I knew that the monster would be the star, and I knew I was worth a little more than just to support a praying mantis." Reason asked to be released from his contract to do the film.

Universal had no difficulty finding other actors willing to act in the shadow of a monster praying mantis. The film would eventually be cast with Craig Stevens in the lead as Colonel Joe Parkman, William Hopper as Dr. Ned Jackson, and Alix Talton as Marge Blaine.

THE GROUND OBSERVER CORPS

In 1952, the U.S. government launched a twenty-four-hour plane-spotting service manned by civilian volunteers called the Ground Observer Corps. Civilian spotters were considered vital to protecting the country against potential Soviet air attacks. Although the government had built many radar networks, low-flying planes could possibly slip through undetected.

However, the service was continually understaffed. In 1954, the *New York Times* reported that there were fewer than 350,000 volunteers, when there was a need for at least 500,000. The lack of volunteers was long attributed to the U.S. Air Force's inability to sell the public on the need to continuously watch the skies. The military jumped on the chance to supply footage of civilian spotters watching the sky. Some critics have called *The Deadly Mantis* propaganda for the Ground Observer Corps. At the end of *The Deadly Mantis,* the Ground Observer Corps is thanked for its cooperation.

Despite being included in the film, the Ground Observer Corps did not survive for very long past the box office release of *The Deadly Mantis.* The movie was released in May 1957. In November 1957, the *New York Times* reported that all Ground Observer Corps posts would be closed by the end of that year.

Alix Talton, William Hopper, and Craig Stevens *(left to right)* in a scene from *The Deadly Mantis*. After finishing *The Deadly Mantis*, Talton, Hopper, and Stevens went on to have very different careers in show business.

CRAIG STEVENS

Craig Stevens was never a major movie star, but he did play many film roles during the 1940s and 1950s. Later in his career, Stevens became quite famous for playing the lead in the groundbreaking television detective show *Peter Gunn,* which ran from 1958 to 1961. As the title character, Stevens created a new image for private detectives: men who were cool and sophisticated instead of tough and gritty. He also starred in 1956's *The Bad Seed*, a well-regarded suspense film about a homicidal little girl; and 1974's *Killer Bees*, another insect monster movie.

WILLIAM HOPPER

William Hopper was in numerous films from the 1930s through the 1950s, including Nathan Juran's *20 Million Miles to Earth*. The best-known movie he appeared in is 1950's *Rebel Without a Cause*, which starred James Dean and Natalie Wood. Hopper also had a major role on *Perry Mason*, a classic television series about a Los Angeles lawyer that ran from 1957 to 1966.

ALIX TALTON

A former Miss Georgia, Alix Talton played supporting roles in only a few movies. Her best-known film is *Rock Around the Clock*, a 1956 movie about the fictional discovery of rock and roll. The first full-length rock-and-roll movie, the film was banned in many countries after teenagers rioted and otherwise caused public disturbances in their excitement over the soundtrack.

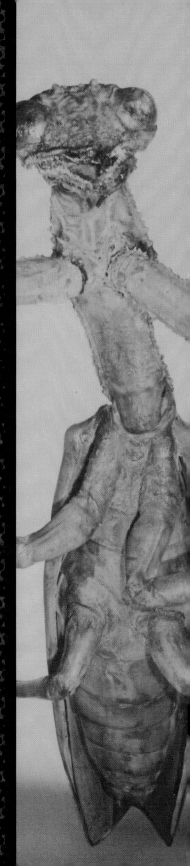

CHAPTER 3

BEHIND THE DEADLY MANTIS

The Deadly Mantis was released by Universal Studios, which is famous for producing some of the best monster movies ever made. Most of these were made in the 1930s and 1940s. The films were sometimes based on classic literature, such as *Dracula* (1931), which is based on the 1897 novel by Bram Stoker, and *Frankenstein* (1931), based on the 1818 novel by Mary Wollstonecraft Shelley.

THE TEEN AUDIENCE

The number of television sets in American homes rose from about 6 million in 1950 to 60 million in 1960. The increasing number of people watching television meant that fewer adults sought entertainment at movie theaters.

However, teenagers were still going to the movies. In the 1950s, the majority of movie-goers were between the ages of twelve and twenty-five. By 1958, the United States had more than 4,000 drive-in theaters, which were very popular with teens.

A helicopter hovers over a giant ant in the movie *Them!*, a highly influential film that inspired a number of giant-insect movies. *Them!* was originally going to be filmed in 3-D, but doubts about the film's money-making potential at the box office did away with that idea.

Film studios realized that they needed to make movies that would appeal to a young audience. During the 1950s, science fiction and horror films were very popular with teenagers. No matter how bad the plots, special effects, and acting were in these movies, the kids flocked to see them anyway.

In his 2003 book, *Hollywood Horror: From Gothic to Cosmic*, author Mark A. Vieira reports that, in 1958, a *Newsweek* magazine poll of theater owners showed that horror movies were the biggest draw. The theater owners said that the monster movies held teenagers' attention better than any other kind of movie.

Vieira also reports that this was true even if the horror movie was so bad it was laughable. Famous monster-movie director Bert I. Gordon is quoted in Vieira's book as saying, "The movie audience these days consists almost entirely of teenagers. Either they're naïve and go to get scared, or they're sophisticated and enjoy scoffing at the pictures."

INSECT FEARS

Atomic fears clearly helped fuel the wave of 1950s movies about mutant bugs. However, people's inherent fear of insects makes it easy to view them as monsters.

Except for those that bite or sting, most insects do not deserve the negative reaction they get from most people, says Gene DeFoliart, University of Wisconsin emeritus professor of entomology, in a *National Wildlife* article. He explains that humans' fear of insects is possibly "a protective mechanism, a genetic holdover from a time when humans were still learning which insects were dangerous."

Locusts—large grasshoppers that are in the same insect family as the praying mantis—are among the few insects that have been dangerous to humankind. According to the United States Agency for International Development (USAID), desert locusts eat their own weight in food each day. This means that, in just twenty-four hours, a small swarm of locusts can consume enough food to feed 2,500 people. Although swarms of locusts destroy crops and often contribute to famine, they are not known to attack people directly.

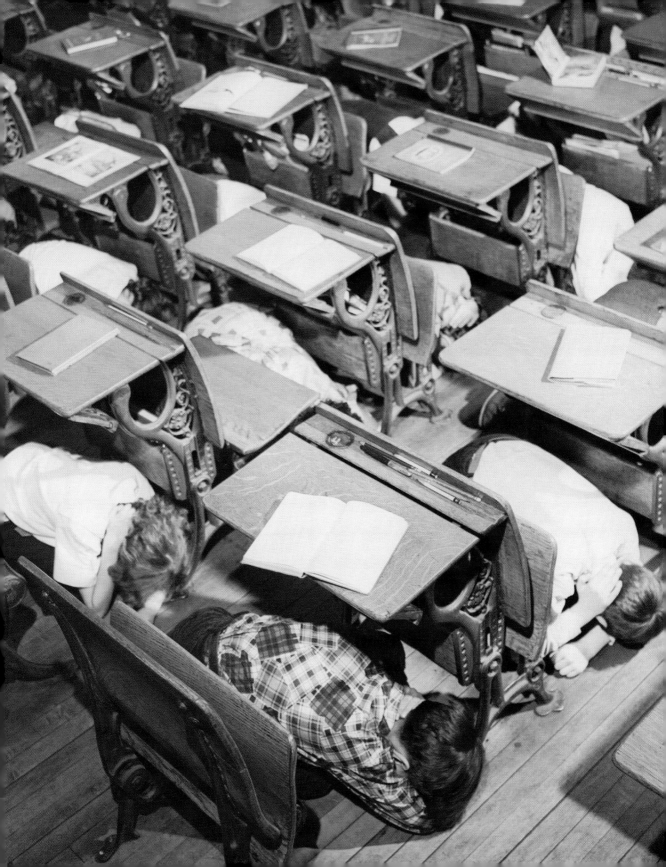

THE ATOMIC AGE

The 1950s were a scary time for teenagers and adults alike. Not long before, in August 1945, the United States dropped atomic bombs on the Japanese cities of Hiroshima and Nagasaki during World War II. The bombs killed at least 100,000 people, sickened (and later killed) many more survivors, and caused widespread structural damage to the cities. The world had never seen destruction of this magnitude before.

Nearly a decade later, in early 1954, Japan suffered another nuclear tragedy when a Japanese fishing boat came too close to an American test of a still mightier nuclear bomb. The test blast was far more powerful than expected. It showered the boat, which was 85 miles (135 km) away, with radioactive ash. Even though the fishermen were not killed by the blast, they soon became ill with radiation poisoning. Several of the fishermen eventually died as a result of the incident, and the tragedy sparked an international outcry against nuclear testing.

The field of nuclear science moved quickly, and it wasn't long before nuclear weapons were on the minds of all Americans. The power of atomic energy was both amazing and terrifying, and soon people's fears were reflected in horror movies. The science fiction films of the 1950s often featured monsters created by nuclear experiments or accidents.

School children perform a duck-and-cover drill in their classroom during the 1950s. Drills like these were intended to protect children from the harmful effects of a nuclear explosion. During the Cold War, many people built bomb shelters for their families in case of a nuclear attack on the United States.

Many believe *The Beast from 20,000 Fathoms* began the wave of such movies. In that 1953 film, an Arctic nuclear test wakes up a "rhedosaurus" (a fictional dinosaur) trapped in ice. The dinosaur swims to New York City, where it causes havoc on Wall Street before dying in a battle at the Cyclone, a famous roller coaster in Coney Island, New York.

"The Beast was a creature of the unknown," said the movie's famous animator, Ray Harryhausen, in a *Virginia Quarterly Review* article. "That was a period in history when no one really knew what would happen with the radiation from an atomic blast."

The most famous atomic age monster is Godzilla, another dinosaur awoken by nuclear blasts. The movie *Godzilla* was released in 1956. Numerous other nuclear monsters were the subject of 1950s movies, such as a monstrous octopus in

CLIMBING IN KING KONG'S FOOTSTEPS

The deadly mantis was not the only movie monster to scale a landmark. Several movies have shown monsters climbing or attacking famous structures over the years. The most famous of these is *King Kong*.

In the original 1933 film, the giant gorilla climbs the Empire State Building in New York City. This scene has inspired many monster movie imitations. In the 1955 movie *It Came from Beneath the Sea*, a giant octopus attacks San Francisco's Golden Gate Bridge. Two years later, in *Beginning of the End*, monster grasshoppers climb the Wrigley Building in Chicago. Although these special effects were novel for the time, they are not very impressive today.

A mushroom cloud rises into the sky while the soldiers of the Eleventh Airborne Division watch from a distance. The atomic explosion was part of a military exercise that took place on November 1, 1951, in the Nevada desert. The very first atomic test took place on July 16, 1945, in New Mexico.

1955's *It Came from Beneath the Sea,* and a massive human in 1957's *The Amazing Colossal Man.*

THE COLD WAR

In 1949, the Soviet Union had developed and tested its own nuclear weapon. This created a great deal of tension during

New York pedestrians take cover in a subway station during a 1951 air raid drill. The drills began with a piercing air raid siren. People would then quickly find shelter. These exercises were part of everyday life during the height of the Cold War.

the Cold War (1947–1991), a long period of hostility between the United States and the Soviet Union.

For decades afterward, there was a great deal of mistrust between non-Communist countries, such as the United States, and Communist countries, such as the Soviet Union. Each side was convinced that the other might launch an attack, so both sides began to build up their stock of nuclear weapons. Both countries also invested heavily in constructing systems that would allow them to launch missiles quickly should the other side strike first.

Afraid that the Soviets would attack across the Arctic Circle and Canada, the United States built an elaborate system of radar networks in the 1950s. These included the DEW line featured in *The Deadly Mantis*. The American military hoped that the warning of a coming attack provided by these radar networks would give them enough time to launch a counterattack.

Many of these military systems are featured in *The Deadly Mantis*. The mantis itself can even be seen as a symbol of Soviet attack. It originates in the Arctic Circle, the area from which the Soviets were expected to attack. The monster even heads straight to Washington, D.C., the political and military capital of the United States.

Many monster movies produced during the Cold War featured creatures that could only be stopped by the military. The majority of these creatures were gigantic monstrosities that had been created by atomic explosions or radiation. In the face of a possible atomic conflict with a competing superpower, old-fashioned monsters like Dracula and the Frankenstein monster no longer seemed as frightening.

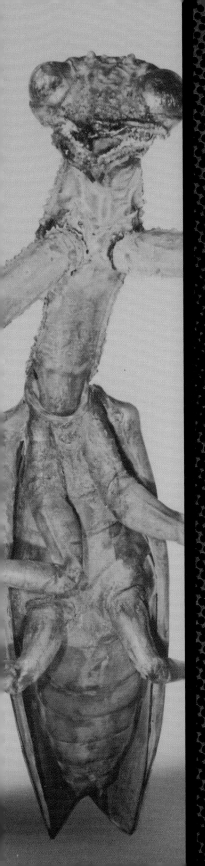

CHAPTER 4

THE DEADLY MANTIS
PHENOMENON

When *The Deadly Mantis* opened in May 1957, *Variety* magazine reported that the film's thrills were tame given the potential of the subject matter. The review blamed this on a derivative script, tedious exposition, slow plot development, and the frequent use of stock footage.

Taken by itself, *The Deadly Mantis* likely would have been lost to time. The movie is not particularly noteworthy in terms of its story, acting, or special effects. However, its similarities to other monster movies from the 1950s and 1960s have ensured it a certain degree of immortality. While *The Deadly Mantis* may not have been a remarkable film, it featured a remarkable monster. The deadly mantis in the film has become one of a number of iconic horror monsters. Along with other movies featuring large insects and prehistoric creatures, *The Deadly Mantis* has developed a cult following. Although it received a tepid response when it was originally released in theaters, the movie was a strong seller when finally released on video in 1996—nearly forty years later.

MONSTER BUGS AND SPIDERS

The Deadly Mantis was one of several 1950s movies featuring oversized insects and arachnids. After the public flocked to go see *Them!*'s gigantic ants, movie studios rushed to produce a number of knockoffs.

The first such film to be released was 1955's *Tarantula*. Its story centers on an ordinary tarantula that grows into a 100-foot (30 meters) monster after it is injected with a special nutrient formula. The enormous spider then escapes from the laboratory and stalks an Arizona town. For the movie, Universal director Jack Arnold used air jets to steer a living tarantula over a miniature landscape. This footage was then combined with shots of the actors in the Mojave Desert. *Tarantula* turned out to be the fifth-biggest moneymaker of 1955.

A 1955 movie poster for *Tarantula*, directed by Jack Arnold. The film features a tarantula that, after receiving a special injection, grows to a tremendous size and goes on a rampage. Although it thrilled and terrified audiences, *Tarantula* was very similar to other giant bug films of the era.

Two other movies about enormous bugs premiered in 1957, the same year that *The Deadly Mantis* was released. The first was a film called *The Black Scorpion*, by special-effects master Willis O'Brien. In this movie, volcanic eruptions free monster scorpions from their underground caverns. The scorpions then terrorize Mexico City. *The Black Scorpion* borrowed heavily from earlier science fiction movies. In fact, the sound effect used for the scorpions' chirps was the same sound effect used for the ants in *Them!*. The movie also used a spider model left over from a deleted sequence in *King Kong,* which O'Brien had previously worked on.

Beginning of the End features a close relative of the praying mantis: the grasshopper. In this film, grasshoppers grow to a monstrous size after eating radioactive vegetables, and then they attack Chicago. Director Bert I. Gordon, working with a low budget, filmed living grasshoppers crawling on postcards of the city's skyline. This made for some laughably strange effects, as the grasshoppers sometimes appear to step off the buildings and walk on air.

The following year saw the release of *Earth Vs. the Spider*, another Bert I. Gordon picture. In the movie, a giant spider is found in a cave and killed. However, the town makes the mistake of storing the spider's body in the high school gym. A noisy rock concert awakens the arachnid, which then attacks the town.

A giant spider sends townspeople fleeing in this still from 1958's *Earth Vs. the Spider*. The film was originally called *The Spider*, but a more dramatic (if somewhat inaccurate) title was decided upon. Director Bert I. Gordon was famous for making movies featuring giant monsters.

The 1950s also saw several monster movies in which humans are transformed into insects. In the 1958 movie *The Fly*, a scientist's experiment with the transmission of matter goes horribly wrong. His matter becomes merged with that of a fly that accidentally gets into the teleportation machine. Critically and financially successful, *The Fly* was followed the next year by *Return of the Fly*, in which the scientist's son repeats his father's mistake. Also released in 1959 was *The Wasp Woman*, the story of a woman who changes into a killer wasp as a result of an experimental youth serum gone awry.

THE INSECT FEAR FILM FESTIVAL

Insects have long played starring roles in horror movies. However, whether a movie features giant bugs, it also usually features some pretty bad science.

That is why the University of Illinois at Urbana-Champaign started the Insect Fear Film Festival. Since 1984, the festival has given audience members an opportunity to "meet" living insects, watch classic insect horror films, and learn more about bug biology.

Each year, the festival has a biological theme. For example, *The Deadly Mantis* was a chosen feature for a festival with the theme of orthopteroid insects, which include crickets, grasshoppers, and cockroaches. One festival was an all-spider event and illustrated how arachnids differ from insects. Yet another festival included only monster movies featuring flies.

The university's entomology department is always adding new twists on the event. In 1994, the festival began serving insect treats, such as deep-fried waxworms, stir-fried silkworm pupae, and lollipops with maguey worms in the center. For a festival on mosquitoes, the department coordinated a theme-appropriate blood drive.

Japanese films such as *Godzilla* (1956) and *Mothra* (1961), which featured giant monsters, were a big hit in the United States. The Japanese poster for *Mothra (left)* contrasts with the American poster for the same film *(right)*. Since 1961, a number of films starring the giant moth have been released.

Monster movies featuring enormous insects and spiders did not stop with the end of the 1950s. In 1961, Japan's *Mosura* (retitled *Mothra* for its American release) chronicled the attack on Japan by a gigantic moth attempting to free its tiny human friends. In 1977, *Empire of the Ants* featured ants mutated to gigantic proportions by toxic waste. And in 2002, *Eight-Legged Freaks* told the tale of a town overrun with giant spiders mutated by chemical waste.

PREHISTORIC CREATURES REVIVED

The Deadly Mantis also followed another 1950s and 1960s monster-movie trend: the reawakening of a prehistoric beast that rampages through modern society.

The Beast from 20,000 Fathoms (1953) started this trend, and *Godzilla* (1956) soon followed. In the 1957 movie

BAD SCIENCE

While the idea of prehistoric creatures being awakened from an icy slumber is popular in film, it is hardly realistic. This is because when most living creatures are frozen, ice crystals form around their blood cells, causing fatal damage.

However, there are a few modern insects that can survive freezing as part of their life cycle. For example, the European corn boarer can stand being about 90 percent frozen in order to survive the winter as a pupa. The arctic wooly bear caterpillar and a tiny fly-like midge in Antarctica can also survive freezing. Both have proteins in their blood that prevent crystals from forming, allowing them to safely freeze and then thaw when ground conditions become more favorable.

The biology in *The Deadly Mantis* is not very accurate. In the movie, the giant mantis is unexpectedly trapped in a glacier, not simply frozen for the winter. No creature could be expected to survive an ice age of indeterminate length.

Another impossibility of the movie's plot is the sheer size of the mantis and the notion that it lived in a world where the smallest insects were as large as men. True, insects were certainly once much larger than they are now, but insects never grew as large as humans. In fact, an insect's exoskeleton would collapse under its own weight if it were the size of a person.

David Arquette encounters an arachnid adversary in 2002's *Eight-Legged Freaks*. The movie was a parody of giant bug films such as *Them!* and *The Deadly Mantis*. In this film, a small town is invaded by spiders that have grown extremely large after being exposed to a toxic chemical spill.

The Monster That Challenged the World, an earthquake releases huge prehistoric sea mollusks that attack California. And in the 1960 movie *Dinosaurus*, undersea explosions near a Caribbean island awaken a frozen tyrannosaurus, brontosaurus, and Neanderthal man.

As with gigantic insects and spiders, prehistoric creatures would continue to terrorize modern society on screen after the

1950s and 1960s. For example, in the 1993 movie *Jurassic Park*, dinosaurs created from prehistoric DNA break through a security system to hunt the people at a theme park. There is something fascinating about large, seemingly unstoppable monsters. No matter what form they take, giant monsters continue to be very popular among fans of horror movies today.

FILMOGRAPHY

The Deadly Mantis (1957). An original theater poster reads, "The most dangerous monster that ever lived! Out of a million years ago . . . a thousand tons of horror!"

Besides the *The Deadly Mantis*, there have been a number of movies dealing with giant bugs.

Them! (1954). The idea for *The Deadly Mantis* came from this film about giant ants mutated by radioactive testing. A critical success and a big moneymaker for Warner Brothers, *Them!* spawned numerous imitators.

Tarantula (1955). A tarantula turns into a 100-foot monster after it is injected with a special nutrient formula. It then escapes from the laboratory and stalks an Arizona town. *Tarantula* was the fifth-biggest moneymaker in 1955.

Beginning of the End (1957). After eating radioactive vegetables, grasshoppers grow to a monstrous size and attack Chicago. Low-budget director Bert I. Gordon filmed the movie using living grasshoppers crawling on postcards, which made for some infamously bad special effects.

The Black Scorpion (1957). Volcanic eruptions release monster scorpions from underground caverns to terrorize Mexico City. The scorpions' chirps were the exact same sounds made by *Them!*'s ants.

The Spider (1958). Another monster movie from low-budget director Bert I. Gordon, this film was also known as *Earth Vs. the Spider*. In the movie, a giant spider awakened by loud music attacks a small town.

Mothra (1961). From the makers of *Godzilla*, this Japanese monster movie features a gigantic moth attacking Tokyo in order to free its tiny human friends.

Killer Bees (1974). Craig Stevens, who played Colonel Joe Parkman in *The Deadly Mantis*, was in this television movie about a deadly swarm of bees.

The Giant Spider Invasion (1975). A black hole allows enormous, man-eating spiders from another dimension to escape into Wisconsin.

Empire of the Ants (1977). This is yet another low-budget monster movie from Bert I. Gordon. This time, a sleazy real estate saleswoman sells property on a remote island controlled by ants that have been mutated by toxic waste.

Eight-Legged Freaks (2002). In this horror-comedy starring David Arquette and Scarlett Johannson, a town is overrun with giant poisonous spiders mutated by chemical waste.

GLOSSARY

appendage An extension of the body, such as an arm, leg, tail, antenna, or fin.

arachnid An animal with eight legs, a hard external skeleton, and a body divided into two parts. Spiders, ticks, and scorpions are all arachnids.

atomic Of or relating to atoms or nuclear energy. An atomic weapon creates a tremendous explosion by splitting an atom.

Cold War An intense ideological struggle and rivalry between the United States and the Soviet Union following World War II.

Communist Based on an economic and governmental system where all property is public.

cult A group of people greatly devoted to a person, idea, or work. Cult movies tend to not make very much money at the box office, but they attract a small, dedicated group of fans.

derivative Unoriginal or imitative.

drive-in theater An outdoor establishment popular in the 1950s where people could watch a movie while sitting in their cars.

entomology The study of insects.

exposition The part of a story that establishes its meaning or purpose.

Ground Observer Corps Nonmilitary volunteers who monitored the skies over the United States for enemy planes in the 1950s.

insatiable Impossible to satisfy.

naïve Lacking worldly experience and understanding.

paleontologist A scientist who studies the life of past geological periods based on fossilized plants and animals.

propaganda Materials promoting specific ideas or views that are usually political in nature.

pseudonym A false name.

voracious Exceedingly hungry.

FOR MORE INFORMATION

American Film Institute
2021 N. Western Avenue
Los Angeles, CA 90027-1657
(323) 856-7600
Web site: http://www.afi.com/

Insect Fear Film Festival
Entomology Department
University of Illinois at Urbana–Champaign
320 Morrill Hall
505 S. Goodwin Avenue
Urbana, IL 61801
(217) 333-2910
Web site: http://www.life.uiuc.edu/entomology/egsa/ifff.htm

WEB SITES

Due to the changing nature of Internet links, the Rosen Publishing Group, Inc., has developed an online list of Web sites related to the subject of this book. This site is updated regularly. Please use this link to access the list:

http://www.rosenlinks.com/famm/dema

FOR FURTHER READING

Brunas, John, Michael Brunas, and Tom Weaver. *Universal Horrors: The Studio's Classic Films, 1931–1946*. Jefferson, NC: McFarland & Company, 1990.

Hancock, Kate. *Science Fiction Films*. New York, NY: Crestwood House, 1991.

Powers, Tom. *Horror Movies*. Minneapolis, MN: Lerner Publications, 1989.

Powers, Tom. *Movie Monsters*. Minneapolis, MN: Lerner Publications, 1989.

Skal, David J. *The Monster Show: A Cultural History of Horror*. London, England: Faber & Faber, 2001.

BIBLIOGRAPHY

"Air Force Closing Observer Posts: Shifts Civilian Ground Unit to Ready Reserves; Cites Advances in Radar." *New York Times*, November 15, 1957.

Baldwin, Hanson W. "Skywatch Two Years Old: Observer Corps Is Vital to Defense Because Radar Has Its Limitations." *New York Times*, July 15, 1954.

Berenbaum, May. Head of Entomology Department, University of Illinois at Urbana-Champaign. Phone interview, August 24, 2005.

Buckley, Tom. "The 'King' of 'Kongs' Reels Again." *New York Times*, August 20, 1976.

Davis, Jill. "When Bugs Go Bad." *Popular Mechanics*, January 2005, Vol. 182, No. 1, p. 27.

"*The Deadly Mantis*: Unimaginatively Executed Science Fiction 'Thriller' Pretty Tame." *Variety*, March 27, 1957.

Garnett, John. "Face to Face with Armageddon." *History Today*, March 1, 1999.

Jensen, Paul M. *The Men Who Made the Monsters*. New York, NY: Twayne Publishers, 1996.

Kuznik, Frank. "Revenge of the Bugs 101." *National Wildlife*, February 12, 1995.

"L.A. Limping: Mantis-Kremlin OK." *Variety*, May 8, 1957.

McCommons, James. "Bug-Eating Machines." *Organic Gardening*, May 1, 2001, Vol. 48, No. 4, p. 71.

Nichols, Peter M. "Home Video: Horror Videos, Including Those with Charismatic Monsters, Are Riding High." *New York Times*, March 22, 1996.

"Predicting Pests." *Weatherwise*, March/April 2005, Vol. 58, No. 2, p. 11.

Ronan, Thomas P. "British Rattled by Rock 'n' Roll." *New York Times*, September 12, 1956.

Ryfle, Steve. "Godzilla's Footprint." *Virginia Quarterly Review*, January 1, 2005, Vol. 81, No. 1, p. 44.

Shaolin Gung Fu Institute. "Northern Praying Mantis Kung Fu." Retrieved August 26, 2005 (http://www.shaolin.com/n_mantis_martialarts.aspx).

Vieira, Mark A. *Hollywood Horror: From Gothic to Cosmic.* New York, NY: Harry N. Abrams, 2003.

Weaver, Tom. *Attack of the Monster Movie Makers: Interviews with Twenty Genre Giants*. Jefferson, NC: McFarland & Company, 1994.

INDEX

ABOUT THE AUTHOR

Genevieve Rajewski is an author who also writes about entertainment and popular culture for magazines and newspapers, including the *Boston Globe*, the *Boston Phoenix*, the *Christian Science Monitor*, and the *Old Farmer's Almanac*.

PHOTO CREDITS

Cover, pp. 1, 4, 6, 9, 11, 13, 14, 17, 19, 21, 22, 30, 32, 37 © Photofest; p. 15 Jim Foster/Corbis; pp. 24, 27, 28 © Bettmann/Corbis; pp. 31, 35, © Everett Collection

Designer: Thomas Forget